Published in Great Britain 1985 by Crown Books.
CLB 1367
Crown Books is a registered imprint of Colour Library Books Ltd.
© 1985 Illustrations and text: Colour Library Books Ltd.,
   Guildford, Surrey, England.
Display and text filmsetting by Acesetters Ltd.,
   Richmond, Surrey, England.
Produced by AGSA, in Barcelona, Spain.
Printed and bound in Barcelona, Spain by Rieusset and Eurobinder.
All rights reserved.
ISBN 0 86283 320 5

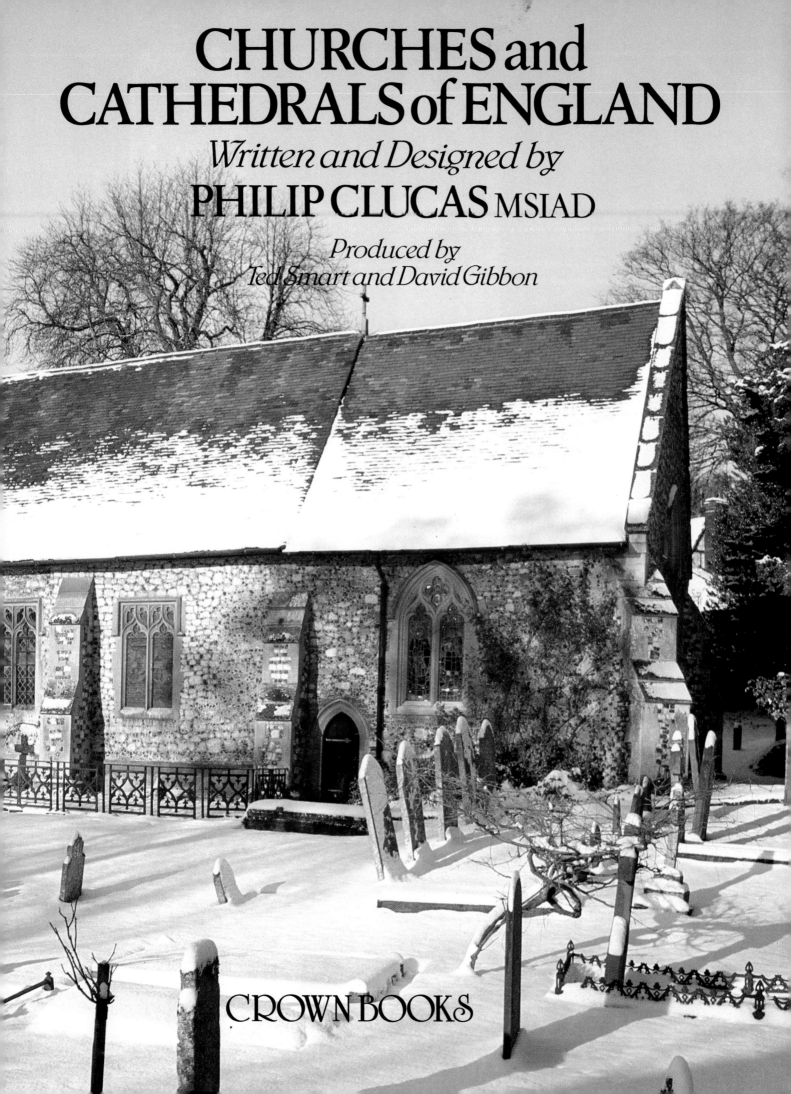

CHURCHES and CATHEDRALS of ENGLAND

Written and Designed by

PHILIP CLUCAS MSIAD

Produced by
Ted Smart and David Gibbon

CROWN BOOKS

INTRODUCTION

For richness and splendour the landscape and architecture of England are unsurpassed and unequalled anywhere in the world. The visual scene is still dominated by our parish and cathedral churches – their power simply as images, their magnificent variety, their enchanting detail, compel attention and demand a reverent sense of awe. On a spiritual level their continuity of religious service links us today with our medieval and Anglo-Saxon forefathers in an unbroken line of observance that may, in some instances, embrace the earliest period of the Celtic and Roman missions.

Some ten thousand medieval churches adorn our land and each has to offer its own unique quality and treasures – be it the massive splendours of our cathedral and monastic foundations – raised to create on earth a reflection of God's heaven – or the simple beauty of a small village church whose green path between the weathered inscriptions on moss-grown leaning headstones – enmeshed in briar and sweet eglantine – leads from the light and sunshine into the solemn, brooding presence of the nave, where the silent air is chill and dank – yet all is warmed and bathed by the stillness of the centuries.

High or humble, each church has the power to dazzle the eye and haunt the mind: these 'jewels' of national heritage are prayers in stone, raised on high by the sons of God – who drew their strength and resolve from implicit faith – to the eternal glory of their Father above. Thus, by its very nature, Romanesque and Gothic architecture speaks to the soul alone – in ornate and elaborate carvings, in sumptuously enriched and coloured glass, and in the very shape and construction of the building. No other age could have furnished so great a majesty (although Victorian Gothic was an interesting attempt at its revival); confidently expressing the belief that the glory due to the Lord should not be tarnished by the squalor of His house. Clearly it is impossible to encapsulate the whole field of their art, yet the parish churches and cathedrals presented within this book represent that unique pinnacle to which the spirit may be uplifted.

The approach is firstly and properly a visual one, accompanied by a comprehensive text which seeks to set each of the selected churches – whether cathedral or parochial – against the backcloth of history and architecture, of religious observance and ritual requirement. Such was the hold of Christ upon the hearts of men that the fabric of England's churches is woven from the warp and woof of life – a rich tapestry that starts with the earliest Celtic fanes, and reaches its glorious climax with the full-blown flowering of Perpendicular architecture, that most uniquely English of all the Gothic styles. Within the thousand year span encompassed by these two extremes (and brought to a close by the Reformation in the 1540s) is a procession of changing emphases and styles – indeed, there is not a stage in the whole architectural evolution which does not offer overwhelming experiences. Who that has seen the Saxon minster at Brixworth, or viewed the unbuttressed towers at Barton-on-Humber and Sompting, could remain unmoved by the subtle beauty born of simplicity – of strength held in complete balance? Norman architecture is equally magnificent and sturdy – as witness Durham's nave where the immense pillars deeply channelled with zig-zag, spirals and chevrons, are as broad as the openings – or at the tiny Romanesque churches of Kilpeck, Barfreston and Iffley, which display a host of wildly lavish Norman sculpture that owe more to pagan mythology than to the Faith. Transitional and Early English architecture saw the introduction of the Gothic pointed arch, which raised vaults on high, and swept arcades forever upwards – Salisbury's unity and Canterbury's peerless Trinity are masterpieces of this style. Wells and Exeter exemplify the florid emphasis of the Decorated period: and the Perpendicular style – the last florescence of the Gothic spirit which speaks of an England rich enough to spend profusely in reverent opulence, and sought at its best to convey splendour and regularity, airy lightness and immensity. With the coming of the Renaissance and its intellectual and religious upheaval, the Church lost much of its ascendancy, yet despite the subsequent ravages of iconoclasts and 'restorers' much remains to us of this glorious heritage. England's churches are thus the highest expressions of the art and architecture of their age – the visual evidence of a triumphant striving to create a paragon of beauty for a lofty and noble purpose.

Opposite page; the Early English chancel at Cobham Church in Kent. Above, a detail of the Perpendicular carved rood-screen at Newton St Margaret's, Hereford.

stone in the watermeads of the River Avon – where grew *'lilies, roses and violets among the many crystal springs, as pure as gold'* – to the completion of the cathedral in 1258, took but thirty-eight years – a surprisingly short period of time for such a monumental task. Having been raised to the glory of God, the geometrical shapes of its masses culminated the following century in the erection of the famous cathedral spire. It is Salisbury's most splendid feature, and its exceptional height expresses a combination of strength and the ascetic striving of the peculiarly medieval desire to lay claim to heaven.

The nave, transepts, Trinity chapel and choir (5) were all completed by the year 1258. In comparison with the grace of Salisbury's exterior (1) the cool, balanced cathedral interior may appear slightly 'remote': the watchwords, however, are 'clarity', 'simplicity' and 'harmony'. The idea of using Purbeck marble (one of the hallmarks of Early English architecture) was inspired by the crusaders' reports of the Holy Land's *rich marbled halls*. Its use quickly came into vogue and dark columns of marble appear throughout the building – the only touch of luxury the Salisbury Master allowed himself. There is virtually no naturalistic carving within the cathedral – only severe rounded moulding – and no tracery, merely lancet windows glazed with monochrome grisaille.

After its dedication in 1258 there were but three major additions to Salisbury Cathedral. The period 1263-84 saw the erection of the grandest cloisters in England, and the building of the magnificent chapter-house; both are among the finest of their kind. The latter (3) is 53ft in diameter and has a beautiful vault rising from a slender central column. In 1334, Richard Farleigh raised the cathedral's culminating feature – the crossing tower, crowned by a 404ft high stone spire (the loftiest in England, and the second tallest in Europe) – which acts as a centralising point for the main body of the cathedral.

■ Two other distinctive towers are to be seen at **Stock** (2) in Essex, and at **Mells** (4) in Somerset. The former is a remarkable example of an early tower which supports a timber belfry and spire; whilst the latter is one of the loveliest of the great Perpendicular stone towers.

Early English architecture – the first phase of the Gothic – is fresh, and characterised by a restrained sense of classical simplicity. Nowhere is this feeling of light and elegance more apparent than at **Salisbury Cathedral** (1,3 and 5), the purest example of the style. The building is without rival, for it is the only Gothic cathedral wholly constant in both design and construction – no other has achieved such a pinnacle of unity. It was planned by Bishop Richard Poore in 1220 as a single conception, built upon a virgin site; thus it was neither influenced by the architecture of a previous age, nor was it a piecemeal of styles. From the laying of the foundation

THE DAWN OF FAITH

One of the most striking features of the history of religion is the way in which people have clung to the holy places of their far distant ancestors. Thus it is that a great many churches of Anglo-Saxon and medieval foundation occupy a site long hallowed by heathen cults. Hilltops and man-made burial chambers (1) of the Neolithic and Bronze Ages were favoured places of worship for the pagan Celts and Saxons: in turn these were rededicated to Christ with the success in England of St Augustine's mission – whose instructions from Pope Gregory were *'do not pull down the fanes of*

incumbent that she was banished to her present location near the belfry door.

Another powerful Celtic symbol adopted by the Church was the device of the severed head. The Celts were head-hunters, and set up the skulls of their enemies to guard their sacred places. Today, severed heads in stone can be seen in countless English churches – as at **Brixworth** (4) in Northamptonshire – and are distinguishable by their severed necks from the benign heads of saints on the upper walls.

Interestingly, such pagan imagery, although associated in the

the heathens but destroy their idols, purify their temples with holy water, set forth relics of the saints, and let them become temples of the true God. So that the people will have no need to change their place of concourse.'

One of the most striking examples of Christian occupation of a pagan holy place is at Knowleton in Dorset, where the medieval church was built at the centre of a Neolithic stone circle. In Yorkshire, Fimber church stands on a Bronze Age barrow. Sacred trees (especially yews) and holy wells worshipped by local people, were invariably included within the churchyard and rededicated to Christian saints. At **Braunston** (5) a carving of a Celtic earth mother stands outside the church. It represents one of Pope Gregory's *'Devils'* – a goddess who was worshipped in primitive fertility rites which took place on the site of the church two thousand years ago. The idol originally stood within the building, but her pagan nature so offended one post-Reformation

sun worship, is widely held responsible for the association between the north side of the churchyard and the Devil, and many people still have an aversion to burial in the northern part of the graveyard where the rays of the sun (8 and 9) never reach. At one time this shaded location was unhallowed ground and was used only for the graves of suicides and unbaptised infants.

■ The Kentish church at **Hythe** (2 and 3) has a crypt in which are stacked and arranged on shelves the remains of over four thousand people (3). One theory states that they are the slain of a bloody battle fought here between Britons and Saxons in AD 456, and many of the skulls display clefts, as if inflicted by a weapon. For some reason the relics attract many

'pilgrims' to this unlikely shrine, and some find the need to lay votive offerings – be it a coin or a flower – upon one or other of the assembled collection of skulls.

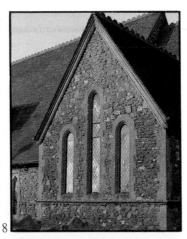

8

9

6

7

10

eyes of medieval Christians with evil, was sought to defend the church against the Devil. On the principle that like cancels out like, grotesque carvings and horrific gargoyles (6) were carved to frighten away malevolent spirits; there was also the idea that to give explicit physical form to the forces of evil was to deprive them of their power. Similarly, mystical symbolism was employed to

restrict supernatural forces – as demonstrated by **Eardisley's** vigorously carved font (7 and 10) where the prominent use of plaitwork was not merely decorative, but had the magical function of ensnaring evil (represented by warriors in combat, with pointed beards and fierce moustaches) and thereby symbolically rendering it harmless.

Another ancient religion, that of

LAPFORD

The hilltop church of **Lapford** (1-6) above the River Yoe in North Devon can trace its foundation back to a Saxon fane, yet the present parish church was built largely at the instigation of one man – Earl William de Tracey. He was one of the four knights to strike down Archbishop Thomas à Becket in his own Cathedral church at Canterbury – the most heinous of medieval deeds, and one that gave England her greatest saint. For his part in the martyrdom, the Earl's property was forfeited and he was ordered to build a certain number of expiatory churches, of which

right across the building, separating the nave (6) from the chancel (4), and divides the north aisle into two portions. Local craftsmen were responsible for the extremely ornate screen, erected in the early years of the 16th century. The outline resembles many of its fellow Devonshire screens, but the enrichments – especially those of the spaces between the ribs of the groining, and the running patterns of foliage and flowers – are perhaps the greatest specimens to be seen anywhere. To add to the splendour, there is a canopy of honour over the Calvary – crossed-ribbed with *roses-en-soleil* in the panels. Where

Lapford was one. Construction commenced in the 1170s and the church was naturally dedicated to St Thomas of Canterbury. By an interesting twist of fate, three hundred and seventy years later King Henry VIII tried to blot out all memory of Becket (who was seen to represent the supreme victory of Church over State), and foundations bearing his name were rededicated – generally to St Thomas the Apostle. Despite intense pressure, however, Lapford and its people courageously refused to bow to royal command: thus the church is one of the rare medieval survivors to have continually honoured the martyr's name.

Lapford church shares with Atherington the reputation of possessing the finest rood screen (1 and 2) in the Kingdom. It extends this ends, the vault of nave and aisle is taken over by a typical 'Devon Cradle', or wagon roof. The church's wealth of carved detail spills over into the magnificently carved bench-ends which display a great variety of devices.

NECTON/SILCHESTER

The church at **Necton** (1,5,6 and 8) in Norfolk, dedicated to All Saints, was built mostly in the 15th century, but the nave arches are from the previous century. The oldest part of the church is St Catherine's chapel on the north side of the chancel: it was founded in 1326 by Lady Maud, widow of Sir Robert de Tony, on condition that a Chantry priest said daily prayers and masses for the soul of her husband, herself and of her father and mother. The medieval idea underlying this was the belief that the time spent in purgatory could be shortened by the prayers and intercessions of the faithful.

1

2

3

Necton's great possession is its fine hammer-beam roof in the nave. The colouring is original and was discovered beneath thick layers of plaster in 1908. The principals are supported by angels (6) with their wings expanded and under them, on pedestals, stand the twelve Apostles with the instruments of their martyrdom in their hands. In the midst of the six on the north side of the nave are effigies of Christ with St Peter, whilst the Virgin Mary stands with St John the Evangelist on the south side. The medieval colouring of the nave vault finds faithful echo in the chancel, where a copy of Sebastian del Piombo's 'Raising of Lazarus' (8) on the reredos adds richness to the high altar.

■ At **Silchester** (4 and 9) colour forms the basis of the church's unique charm, where mellow brick and tile seem to merge as natural forms into a landscape haunted by memories of the lost Roman city of *Callera Atrebatum*.

■ The parish church at **Wisborough Green** (3) in West

4

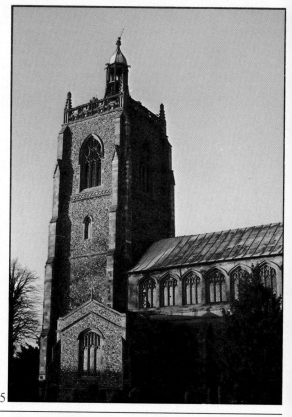

5

weighing more than a ton. It is a contemporary of those at Stonehenge and may originally have been associated with pagan rites. The 'holy stone' was consecrated by the Normans, but was nearly destroyed during the zeal of the Reformation when we read that, *'at the order of Henry VIII St Peter Ad Vincular gave up a crucifix with a drop of the Virgin's milk set in crystal in it; the hair shirt, comb and bones of St James; relics of the Holy Sepulchre and the Mount of Olives; hair of St Peter, stones from St Stephen's martyrdom; and other relics of St Edmund of Canterbury, St Giles, St Sebastian and St Silvester'*. To see such treasures the pious came from far and wide (and bear witness to the general importance of the church in medieval times), but all 'papist shams' were destroyed – 'cleansed' from the church – save for the altar stone which was hidden, and not discovered until 1901.

■ The Lord of the Manor was usually responsible for building the original Norman or medieval

Sussex has a rare dedication to St Peter Ad Vincular (St Peter in Chains) – the same dedication as the chapel abutting the execution ground in the Tower of London. This adds weight to the suspicion that the building was formerly the keep of a castle or stockade. The doorway is 13 feet high and would admit a mounted warrior, whilst the 5 feet thick walls are strong enough to withstand a heavy assault. High on the hill, the church itself suggests an ideal lookout point above the River Arun.

The 13th century chancel has a most unusual altar – a stone

parish church, and at **Corbet** (2) he did so on his own land and near his own house. However, Victorian benefactors were responsible for the present building of St Andrew's at **Okeford Fitzpaine** (7) which was almost entirely rebuilt in 1866. Using the materials of the earlier 14th century church, St Andrew's copied its predecessor's plan and it is thus a fairly faithful and praiseworthy 19th century reproduction of a late-medieval church.

Thaxted Church (1-6) is one of the most magnificent parish churches in the country, and its great size – 183ft long, with a spire (2) of almost equal height – indicates the prosperity of the Essex town in earlier days. It was in fact a centre of the wool trade, and in the mid-14th century was a famous cutlery town. This period saw the beginning of the rebuilding of the church which lasted for over one hundred and seventy years.

Thaxted church rises magnificently above the plastered and half-timbered cottages of the old town and the Guild Hall of the Cutlers. It is dedicated to St John

the Baptist and consists of a narrow nave with much wider aisles – the arcade (6) was built in 1340 – a crossing with north and south transepts (1), and two porches, each with a parvis room above. Over the northern porch is the chapel of Blessed John Bull, the priest martyr and instigator of the Peasants' Revolt of 1381. At the east end of the church, occupying the site of the original Saxon foundation, is Thaxted's spacious chancel (3) in which hang the banners of St Brigid, St Catherine, St James, St Lawrence (Patron Saint of Cutlers), St Thomas of Canterbury and Our Lady. The

3

4

6

latter two saints have side chapels dedicated to their memory flanking the High Altar – the northern Becket chapel being renowned for its painted ceiling and Tudor glass.

The interior of the church – due to its large windows, its clerestory and the use of white paint – is full of light and air (4 and 5). This feeling of spaciousness is further enhanced by the absence of pews and by its 'walls of glass' – where only buttresses and mullions serve to break the glazing. There are good fragments of medieval stained glass remaining, but in general the glass is clear. Overhead, the roof timbers date from c1510 and are vigorously carved with figures of angels and heraldic emblems, whilst on the nave arches are some fine portrait heads wrought from stone. Good craftsmanship is also apparent in the splendid 15th century font-cover, and in the Jacobean pulpit.

CROMPTON BEAUCHAMP/FAIRFORD

Light – the intangible phenomenon by which the world is made visible – has, since time immemorial, been symbolically equated with goodness and revelation, and has therefore been a focal point of the religions of mankind. The flowering of the art of stained glass in the Middle Ages was inspired to *'illumine mens' minds so they may travel through it (light) to an apprehension of God's light'*. At the end of the Saxon era and in Norman times, when the boom in ecclesiastical building was beginning, windows were small, and characterised by large splays which encouraged as much light as

All is of the late-15th and early-16th century (as is the building of this 'wool-church' – the gift of the wool stapler and cloth merchant, John Tame) and is thought to be of the school of Barnard Flower, Master Glass Painter to King Henry VII.

The 'Passion' occupies the east window, but otherwise Fairford begins with Old Testament scenes and continues with the early life of the Virgin, the 'Annunciation', the life of the infant Jesus, and the whole of the Gospel story up to Pentecost. In the clerestory, saints and martyrs occupy the south windows, and face the 'evil'

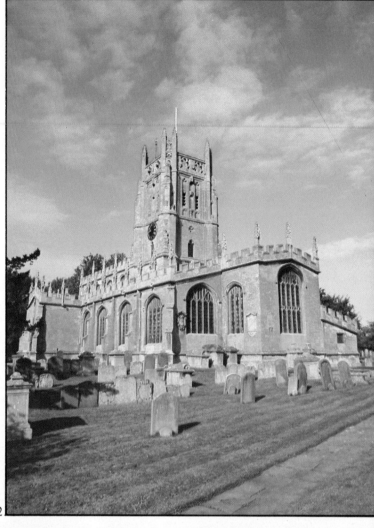

possible to seep into the church – such windows are exemplified by the 13th century chancel-light (3) at **Crompton Beauchamp** (1).

As the art of medieval bar tracery developed, cathedrals and churches became ablaze with the colour of stained glass. Windows gradually increased in size, until some 15th-century churches had the appearance of huge expanses of glass held together by narrow strips of stone. The opportunity offered by these vast areas of glazing was eagerly seized upon by artists, and their jewel-like creations are among the finest possessions of our medieval heritage. Of all England's parish churches, St Mary's at **Fairford** (2,4,5,6 and 7) contains the greatest display of medieval stained glass. As a complete series, the glass in this Gloucestershire church is unique. Its twenty-eight Perpendicular windows cover an area of two thousand square feet. Fairford is, in fact, the Bible in glass: and the whole faith of the Church is presented in vivid colour.

and the artist clearly took enormous delight in the dramatic use of reds and blues. In the fourth light (7) stands St Michael in golden armour. He suspends a pair of scales – in one pan a little soul is being weighed, whilst into the opposite pan a devil has climbed in in an attempt to pervert the balance – the innocent soul is still worthy and will proceed to the left hand side of the window tracery where the blessed, in white robes, file past St Peter up a golden stairway that leads to the heavenly bliss of the upper half of the Great West Window (5). Here, the innocent form the outer bands of worshippers who encircle Christ enthroned upon His tricolour rainbow (a symbol of the Trinity). At Christ's feet kneel His mother and St John the Baptist, while the angelic host surround their heavenly Lord to whom full jurisdiction is given. However, it is the imagery to the right of the arch-angel, in the lower tracery, which attracts most attention, for here the full rein of the artist's imagination has been allowed to run riot. He fills the panels with grotesque and fascinating detail of a hellish nightmare, wherein a blue

5

6

7

northern side, filled to overflowing with those who have persecuted the Church – with a wealth of demons in the traceries. The most spectacular of Fairford's windows – the Great West Window (5,6 and 7) – is given over to the theme of the apocalyptic end of the world, and the judgement of souls. It is the finest example of a 'doom-window'

devil (4) carts off an old man to destruction, and Satan (5) is seen with a fish's head devouring a stream of damned sinners, while his bloated stomach forms a second head with leering yellow eyes and a row of hideously sharp teeth – all bathed in the blood-red glow of hell-fire.

Sited high up on Dartmoor, the church of St Pancras at **Widecombe-in-the-Moor** (1 and 2) overlooks a vast panorama of moorland. It is a setting of incomparable loveliness in all seasons; the distant hills shading to green in spring (1), shimmering purple under summer heather, or enfolded in the white of winter snows. The large, late-14th century church has one of the noblest towers in Devon (2). It is granite at its most glorious and rises for 135ft. Dating from the early-16th century, it was raised at the expense of prosperous tin miners keen to manifest their newly

Germanus and part of the shroud in which his body rested, from the Abbot of St Germains' Convent in Auxerre. The fabric of the church is a lovely, dappled, rust-coloured stone, and the interior has at various times been altered. Much of the recent restoration work has been with a fine sense of the dramatic, and the interior retains a grandly baronial air.

■ The tower and south porch of St Mary's, **Boxford** (5) in Suffolk. The former houses a fine peal of medieval bells, whilst the latter is elaborately carved in stone with the 'Annunciation' at its centre.

acquired wealth. The tower has an interesting story associated with it. In 1638, in the middle of Divine Service, a bolt of thunder – '*with lightning, hail and fire*' – struck the tower, toppling one of its pinnacles, and a great, fiery ball passed right through the choir, killing four people and injuring sixty-two, some of whom died later. One survivor recalled seeing a mysterious traveller at the service who smelt of sulphur and in an unguarded moment exposed a cloven hoof!

■ In 1162 a priory of Augustinian canons was established at **St Germans** (3 and 4) in Cornwall, and it is their monastic building which forms the present parish church. Its west face is Norman, and at its centre is a magnificent, cathedral-like doorway. Through the Romanesque door, looking east, is a lofty nave 25ft wide, and an aisle of equal proportions on the south side, divided by an arcade of six arches (3). It was built in such splendid manner to receive a gift of one small bone of the arm of St

CAWSTON/HUTTOFT

The large flint church of St Agnes at **Cawston** (5,6,9 and 10) is one of Norfolk's finest. Its freestone tower soars for 120ft, to dominate the village and surrounding countryside – with mighty buttresses reaching to the tower's summit. Its mood is sombre and starkly impressive – without parapets its austerity is relieved only by the combination of windows and doorway. The latter displays in its spandrils the carving of a dragon and a 'wild man'. The motif is repeated on the piscina within the church and bears witness to the fact that the De la Pole family – whose crest the

and is renowned for two features – its incomparable nave roof, and the rood screen. The former is of a hammer-beam construction and has carved angels on its projecting beams (6) and cherubs with outspread wings along the cornice. The bosses (5) are magnificently carved, and at the east end are the figures which formerly stood by the great rood. The screen itself (10) is in very good condition, with its original paintings by Flemish artists of the 15th century. It includes among its twenty portraits those of the church's patron saint, St Agnes, with a lamb (reminding us of the connection between

carvings represent – were patrons of the medieval church. Indeed, St Agnes' itself was rebuilt in the 14th century by one prominent member of the House – Michael, the Earl of Suffolk.

His church at Cawston displays both Decorated and early-Perpendicular styles of architecture,

wooden roof of the nave incorporates within its design the sacred monograms of Christ and the encircled letter 'M' of His mother, the Virgin Mary. At the west end of the nave lies Huttoft's greatest possession – its Perpendicular font (4), depicting the Madonna and Child, and the Trinity with the Twelve Apostles in pairs on the bowl, saints on the stem, and the symbols of the four Evangelists at the base.

■ **Pirton Church** (1 and 8) in Worcestershire has a picturesque example of a half-timbered Tudor belltower (1) surmounted by a pyramidal roof of red tiles. These 'magpie' towers are rare, and are only found in districts that were once thickly forested. They are invariably raised in oak with a complex framework filled with 'wattle and daub' – wooden sticks woven in the form of close hurdles and coated in clay mixed with chopped straw. Pirton's tower abuts a Norman nave containing an ancient font and many medieval tiles (8), of which there are two distinct colours – red and ochre – with a fleur-de-lis pattern predominating.

■ 7: A festival of flowers at St John's Church, **Buxton**.

7

Cawston and the Middle Ages' wool industry), St Andrew with his saltire cross (9), and an interesting representation of Sir John Schorne removing a horned imp (symbolizing gout) from his boot – an allusion to Sir John's well at Marsham, the waters of which were much praised as a gout cure.

■ The medieval Lincolnshire church of **Huttoft** (2,3 and 4) possesses a graceful chancel and nave (2) with ancient arcade and clerestory. Contemporary with these are the robustly carved belfry windows (3) and the splendid 14th century chest – panelled throughout with tracery. The

10

WELLS CATHEDRAL

The earliest completely Gothic cathedral in Europe is also one of England's most beautiful. The graceful West Country cathedral of **Wells** (1-13) was begun in 1176, a few years after William of Sens had introduced the new style of architecture at Canterbury. Bishop Reginald de Bohun was greatly influenced by the design and caused the present building at Wells to be raised on a similarly grand scale. His idea that '*the honour due to God should not be tarnished by the squalor of His house*' could well be taken as the sense of harmony (8) is dashed, however, the moment one passes into the nave, by the sudden and unexpected drama of the great inverted 'strainer arch' (3) standing directly ahead and dominating all. It has been likened to a gaping 'hell-mouth' with ascending horns and huge roundels on either side of the intersection looking like glowering eyes. The monumental 'sinew in stone' is thrice repeated – at the nave and at the entry to each of the transepts. It was not planned, but improvised to solve the crisis of the dangerous westerly

dictum of medieval architecture, and here resulted in the construction of a cathedral filled with air, light and space, possessing the typical ribbed vaults and pointed arches that represent the emergence of a purely English style of Gothic Art. Wells Cathedral seems to hold the spirit of the Middle Ages forever in its mellow stonework. The outward

WELLS CATHEDRAL

tilting and cracking of the central tower in 1340.

By the year 1239 the choir and transepts were finished and the nave was suitably advanced for the cathedral to be consecrated. Much of the work was undertaken by Adam Lock, whose influence is everywhere apparent. His piers are at once massive yet delicate – consisting of twenty-four shafts that conceal rather than display the line of upward thrust – and gently lead the eye along the vertical of the nave (6) towards the upper church. The progression is

7

8

9

10

accompanied at every level by a host of carved detail which fills both capital and corbel with some of England's finest sculpture. They not only exemplify marvellous skill, but capture for eternity the humour of the age. Much of the carving depicts scenes from everyday life – two beggars steal apples from an orchard (7) and are apprehended by an angry farmer (9); men are shown toiling in vineyards; a fox makes off with a goose, and a cobbler perpetually mends shoes whilst a poor woman who cannot afford shoes carefully pulls a thorn from her bare foot.

The chapter house was raised during the episcopacy of William de Marchia in 1300, and completed six years later. It is uniquely elevated upon an undercroft (which served as a treasury) and is approached by a marvellous stairway of broad flags which curve up towards a double-arched doorway of miraculous delicacy. The flight (4) – which has been compared to a flowing river – has been worn down through the ages by the tread of countless generations of the faithful. Once inside the Chapter House, a superb marble central pier (10) fans out

through the choir towards the Great East Window – the 'Golden Window', ablaze with the translucent colouring of greens, yellows, and ochre – the comparative simplicity of the Early English nave gives way to the lightness and richness of the high altar which is extremely florid and beautiful, having stone tracery which climbs over every available inch of wall to tangle its tendrils in the fantasy of the roof's net vaulting.

■ At **Broad Hinton** (15) in Wiltshire there is a fine example of a late-Elizabethan tomb showing Sir Thomas Wroughton – at one

into thirty-two ribs. It is the apotheosis of the tierceron vault, which never fails to stir a sense of the marvellous: indeed, it is perhaps the most beautiful of all those polygonal chapter house interiors which are unique to English cathedral architecture.

The Lady chapel (2) – with its incomparable vault (12) and 14th century stained glass (11 and 13) – and the central tower (1: seen to best advantage from the gardens of the Bishop's Palace) were both designed by Thomas Witney during the period 1310-22. The

former is joined to the choir by a rectochoir built by local mason William Joyce; his main work however, was the reconstruction of the cathedral's eastern end, providing the beautiful vista through the open arches to the high altar (5). As one passes

time Sheriff of the County – and his wife Anne. Their heavily stylised effigies kneel in the attitude of prayer, whilst below their feet the diminutive figures of their four sons and four daughters likewise kneel – in humble submission to their parents (14).

HUNSTANTON/WOLVERTON

The church of St Mary, **Hunstanton** (3,5,6 and 7) is a notable example of the early-Decorated style of architecture prevalent in the first quarter of the 14th century. It possesses a fine chancel screen with Tudor panels showing painted figures of the Apostles (6), and a Victorian pulpit (3) of white stone and alabaster, dedicated to the memory of Henry le Strange. Indeed, throughout its history this Norfolk church has been closely associated with the le Strange family, who have lived at the nearby moated mansion of Old Hunstanton for over nine hundred years. Their monuments crowd the church; the finest being the tomb-slab portrait in brass of Sir Roger le Strange (7) in an unusual attitude with hands uplifted and outspread, as if contemplating the '*wonderment of heaven*', and in full knightly panoply, including a tabard with an intricate coat-of-arms. Another brass (5) of 1490, depicts Edmund and his wife, Agnes, in civilian costume. His tight, upper garment resembles a

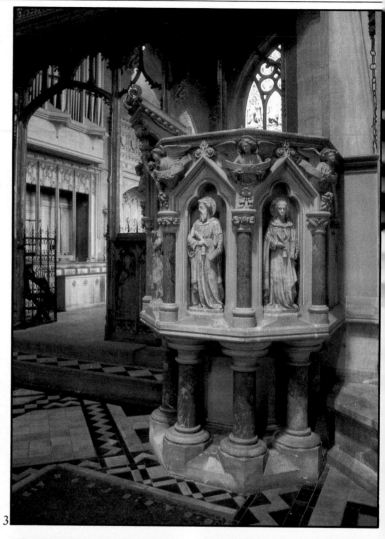

pelisse or surtout with fur around the wrists, whilst his wife wears a head-dress consisting of a perfectly plain bonnet with a veil.

■ In its assured Wren manner the noble, red brick tower of St Catherine's, **Wolverton** (1,2 and 4) contrasts with the low-built church beneath it. Both tower and church were raised in 1717. St Catherine's consists of a nave and north and south transepts – with gracious windows (1) with distinctively pronounced keystones – and a chancel (4) with wrought-iron altar-rails and wooden, carved reredos; both displaying splendid, 18th century workmanship.

BRADFORD-ON-AVON/HALES

The tiny church of St Laurence, **Bradford-on-Avon** (1,3,5 and 6) is one of the very few Anglo-Saxon churches to survive intact – a unique and superb example from pre-Conquest England. It is thought that the church was built by St Aldhelm – the first Bishop of Sherbourne, and a close relative of King Ine of Wessex – who lived in the late 7th century. The plan and

9ft 8ins high by 3ft 6ins wide; the tapering of doorways and arches (a Saxon feature); the three original windows which are splayed on both sides, and the figures of ministering angels hovering with outstretched hands veiled by napkins – no doubt originally on either side of a figure of Our Lord upon the Cross.

Above the tiny altar stand the

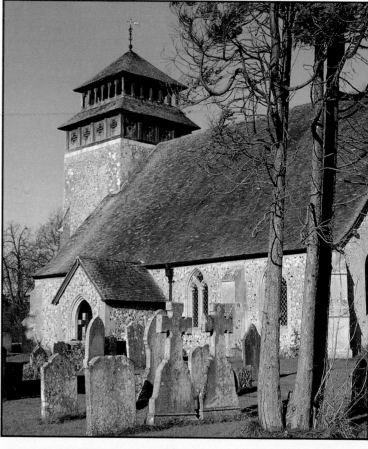

much of the fabric of St Laurence's dates from this early period, but the external decoration is of the late 10th century when the blind arcading of the outside walls (1) was formed by cutting into the stonework of the existing church. This embellishment was probably carried out at the behest of King Ethelred, who chose to hide the relics of his half-brother, St Edward the Martyr (the King murdered at his stepmother's instigation at Corfe Castle in 978) within the church *'that therein might be found a safe refuge – impenetrable confugium* (referring to the dense woods then surrounding Bradford) – *'against the insults of the Danes'*.

After the coming of the Normans, the Saxon church was put to secular use and its true purpose was forgotten. Old deeds reveal the name *'Skull House'* and it is likely that it was used as a charnel house during the Middle Ages, and to this fact St Laurence's owes its preservation in its original state. Rediscovered by chance a century ago, it now stands revealed as one of the oldest and smallest – the height of the nave (6) is greater than its length – churches in the land.

Internally the chief features are the dimensions of the chancel arch,

vertically. The dendrological method of determining age has traced the construction of these wooden walls to the year 845. At this time the whole building – both chancel and nave – was of timber, and its affirmed antiquity makes St Andrew's the oldest surviving wooden church in the world. The dormer windows, the porch and the brick-built chancel were all added during the reign of the Tudors, as was the wooden tower with its small, shingled spire.

5

7

remains of a Saxon cross (5) – one of seven set up by order of Ecquin, Bishop of Worcester, to denote the resting place of St Aldhelm's bier when it was carried from Doulting, where he had died, to his shrine at Malmesbury.

■ Another of England's architectural treasures, the Church of St Andrew at **Greensted-juxta-Ongar** (7) in Essex, also dates from the Saxon era; where the walls of the nave consist of massive oak trunks cleft in half and set

■ The rounded 'apse' – or chancel based on the old basilica plan – is a rare feature which gives a firm indication that a church is of early Norman foundation. One such example is St Margaret's, **Hales** (4) whose stone-built tower and thatched roof are charmingly set among the verdant water-meads of Norfolk.

■ 2. The parish church of **Moonstoke** in Hampshire.

Hereford Cathedral (2,3,4 and 5) owes its foundation to King Offa of Mercia who, in AD 792, was responsible for the murder of St Ethelbert. In expiation he built a costly shrine to receive the body of the martyred East Anglian King. The present cathedral is substantially of Norman date, and to this style belong the columns, arches and triforium of the choir, the great arches under the tower, the columns and arches of the nave, and the font (2) of about 1140 – sculpted from a single block of sandstone with figures of the Apostles occupying each of its twelve niches. Throughout the Middle Ages extensions and partial reconstructions were carried out in the styles fashionable at the time: thus, simply by looking up (5) it is possible to see three great innovations of medieval architecture uniquely positioned one above another: the rounded Norman arch, the Early English pointed arch, and finally, the glorious triumph of the Perpendicular fan vaulting.

The Lady chapel (4), built between 1217 and 1225, has a series of five narrow lancets (unusually elaborate for the period, with thick clustered shafts in the window embrasures) which lend

special dignity to the chapel. Among their glass is a depiction of Christ carrying a crucifix of 'green' wood to Calvary – a touching use of medieval symbolism to illustrate the everlasting power of the cross. In the mid-13th century Hereford was brought to the forefront of fashion by the Savoyard Bishop, Peter Acquablanca who, by building a northern transept, completed the cruciform shape of the present cathedral. His architectural style is perhaps the most lavish – being the most extreme example of that phase of the Decorated style known as 'Geometric'.

■ Raised in 1499, and a masterpiece of Perpendicular architecture, **Bath Abbey** (1) occupies the site of the Saxon abbey in which Edgar was crowned King of the English in 937. Transformed into a vast minster by the Normans, it is now renowned for its huge and elaborate windows and its superlative 16th century fan vaulting (1) designed by William Vertue.

EYE/CLOPHILL/UFFORD

Once surrounded by water, and named after the old Saxon word for 'island', the church of St Peter and St Paul, at **Eye** (2 and 3) in Suffolk, is well known for its splendid 100ft high, 15th century west tower, panelled in flint and stone, with octagonal buttresses. The main body of the church predates the tower by one hundred years, and upon entering one is surprised by its lightness. The effect is mainly due to the clear glass of the clerestory, the relative simplicity of which is augmented elsewhere by the richness of modern stained glass (3). The pre-Reformation screen is the greatest

statues, and terminates in a carved pelican pecking its own breast (6) – the mystical symbol of Christ's sacrifice for mankind upon the Cross. It was carved in 1450 and the elaboration of the pinnacles, canopies and tabernacle work is an astonishing triumph of medieval art, made even more impressive by the fact that the whole work is telescopic, so that when raised the lower parts slide up over the superstructure.

The Ufford font cover was once '*all gilt over with gold*', and enough of the gilding and gesso-work remains to convey some idea of its original appearance. The hammer-

1

treasure at Eye, having fifteen painted panels of saints and kings, and a magnificent rood (2) supported on either side by figures of the Virgin Mary and St John the Baptist, nobly restored by Sir Ninian Comper.

■ Another of Suffolk's famous village churches is the Norman and Perpendicular church of St Mary, **Ufford** (5,6,7 and 8), raised in the typical East Anglian fashion of elaborate flushwork with a pleasant warming relief of well-carved stone (8). As at Eye, it can show incomparable woodwork, and Ufford possesses the finest medieval font cover to be seen. This great Gothic masterpiece is said to be the most beautiful cover in the world – Nuremburg runs a close second. The font itself is plain by comparison, carved with Tudor roses, grotesque faces and heraldic shields of the influential Suffolk families of Willoughby and Ufford. Above the stone font, the cover (5) rises for a staggering 18ft, soaring in graceful receding tiers of canopied niches which once held

3

4

beam roof of the nave – with its carved angels – and the chancel's tie-beam vault also possess much of their original colouring, and in their rafters the sacred monogram 'IHS' and 'MR' (the cypher of Our Lady) are repeatedly painted upon the boards. The chancel roof (7) is unusual in having the arched bracings intersected by pendants halfway up: they bear shields upon which the instruments of Christ's Passion are vividly evoked.

■ The purpose of medieval font-covers – however elaborate – was to protect the holy water of the font from being stolen by witches who used it in their magic rites.

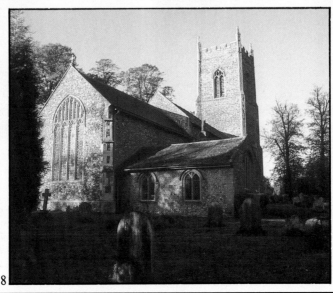

Fantastic as the idea of black rites might appear to the modern mind there are still those who take the opportunity to practise the art. One notorious incident occurred in March 1963 amid the gaunt ruins of St Mary's, **Clophill** (1), whose eerie remains crown the brow of Dead Man's Hill. In this sorry Bedfordshire church, which has been deserted for centuries, the tomb of an apothecary's wife was torn open, and her bones arranged in a circle about the gutted nave. The desecration supposedly served some part of a Black Mass, and an attempt at necromancy.

■ 4: The church at **Beddingham** upon the South Downs of Sussex.

BRIDFORD/FRAMLINGHAM

The granite, Perpendicular church at **Bridford** (1,2,3,4 and 5) lies to the west of the Teign Valley, in the Dartmoor foothills of south Devon. The gentle, time-weathered stone of its ancient fabric (2 and 5) is perhaps a last reminder of mellowness before the harsh moor landscape grips the senses with the bleakness of its grey boulders piled like ramparts and horizons topped by massive, jagged tors. The 15th century church has some late-medieval glass, a fine carved pulpit, stalls, bench-ends, wagon roofs and other notable medieval woodwork. Best of all, however, is Bridford's splendid rood screen (3) of 1508. It is exceptional in possessing small, exquisitely carved figures of Apostles and Prophets (1).

■ The church and churchyard of St Michael's at **Framlingham** (7) in Suffolk are positioned high above the market-place. The nave, with its hammer-beam roof, and the tower (7) are both fine examples of the East Anglian 15th century style.

1

2

3

5

6

■ The parish church of **Castle Ashby** (6) is set within the grounds of the Marquess of Northampton's Elizabethan mansion house landscaped by Capability Brown. The 14th and 15th century church has an attractive tower surmounted by a pyramid roof; and within are many monuments to the Crompton family – owners of the manor. Of particular interest is a brass in the chancel floor of the rector William Ermyn (6), dated 1401. His cope is elaborately decorated with ten saints all standing under traceried canopies on the orphreys. There are coats-of-arms on the morse.

4

IFFLEY

The church of St Mary at **Iffley** (1-10) in Oxfordshire is one of England's most famous Norman churches. It dates from the late-12th century, and was built by the Norman family of St Remy in the reign of King Henry II. It is a Romanesque showpiece, and rightly so, for a wealth of superb Norman ornamentation adorns both the exterior and the interior fabric of the church. It comprises a Norman nave, tower and chancel (probably based upon a two-cell Saxon church). The sanctuary (3) in which the high altar (10) now stands is an extension of the Romanesque chancel. It is a very fine example of 13th century workmanship, with its three single-light lancet windows and slim vault-mouldings springing from compound filleted shafts, in striking contrast to the heavier and more ornate Norman choir (5). The boss at the centre of the choir's multi-chevron (zig-zag), carved ribs of the vault has a *seraph* (7) surrounded by grotesque heads. This fabled creature is one of the

Seraphim; the living creatures with three pairs of wings seen in Isaiah's vision as hovering over the throne of God.

A similarly lively theme is enacted in the moulding of the south doorway (2), whose Romanesque carvings have weathered well because a porch protected them from the 15th century until 1807. On the right hand side of the door are symbols of Good – a knight encouraging his weary companion, and Samson slaying the lion – whilst the left side of the portal shows warnings of Evil – wild beasts overpower tame; King Henry II (among the

6

7

'monsters' for his role in Becket's martyrdom) and a centaur suckling its young (9). The latter, half-human, half-horse, were seen by the Church as pagan figures. Epona's children, they pulled the chariot of the solstice sun.

Iffley's Great West Front (1) displays a most impressive array of Norman decoration, with its deeply-recessed doorway of six superimposed orders without capitals: four are of chevron pattern and two columns are adorned with one hundred and ten beak-heads (6) surmounted by a semicircular hood-mould of medallions linked by lions' heads, among which

8

9

10

symbols of the Evangelists and signs of the zodiac can be identified; all seasons being subject to the Gospels. The richness and originality of this craft is extended to encompass the three top windows of the western gable (8) and the centralised 'Eye of God' window.

Some exquisite fragments of medieval glass remain in the nave and in the southeast window can be seen the arms (4) of John de la Pole, Duke of Suffolk, and great-grandson of Geoffrey Chaucer. A little further along is a blocked up arch which was probably the window through which Annora, a noble anchoress, viewed the altar. The extreme degree of religious observance involved the hermit being walled-up for life within a small cell, which had but one aperture to the high altar, and another prepared in readiness for the grave. Annora lived in her cell at Iffley for nine years, until her death in 1241, during which time she received gifts of clothing and firewood from King Henry III.

ELY CATHEDRAL

Originally a monastery sited on an island in the midst of a vast expanse of marshy Fenland, **Ely Cathedral** (1-5) was founded in AD 673 by St Etheldreda. As mists from the now drained countryside roll in to skirt the lower fabric of the Anglo-Norman silhouette, its immense bulk, divided at intervals by the vertical forms of pinnacles, turrets and buttresses, rises up to haunt the cowled landscape like a shadowed crown against the Fens.

The Norman Abbot, Simeon, was eighty-six years old when appointed to the See in 1083, and from his vision (to create a church worthy of God's presence within it)

medieval passion for geometry created Ely's breathtakingly beautiful star-shaped vault and lantern tower – the octagon – a work of supreme genius (executed by William Hurle, the King's Master Carpenter), and medieval architecture's most original concept. Its essence of spacious boldness epitomises the spirit of the Decorated style. The octagon is a masterpiece of uplifted beauty, where dappled light shafts downwards from the highest windows and is captured within the lantern to be held like a glorious aureola (2) over the whole body of the church.

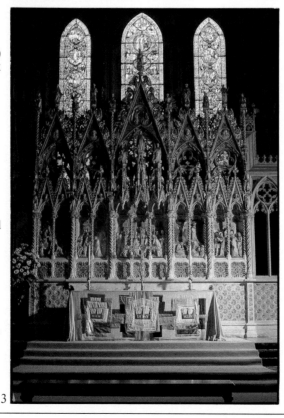

the present cathedral springs. The west front (4) is a notable survivor of the Romanesque minster – as is the magnificent 248ft long nave (5) whose feeling of soaring stonework is created by the exceedingly high triforium: the effect is no mere illusion, however, for Ely's nave is taller than any of its contemporaries. At 86ft in height the walls' tendency to bow ruled out the possibility of a stone vault, and thus the ceiling has always been of the lighter material – wood. Beyond the soaring nave, the presbytery and High Altar (3) were constructed during the period 1234-52 to provide a more sumptuous setting for St Etheldreda's shrine.

In 1322 the Norman crossing tower collapsed *'with a roar like thunder, of shock and so great a tumult'*. Faced with a gaping hole torn from the cathedral's heart, the sacrist decided against rebuilding the tower, and opted instead for the daringly experimental idea of creating an octagon. The choice was indeed fortunate, for the

ST MARY'S WARWICK

The church of St Mary at **Warwick** (1-9) is of Saxon foundation with a Norman crypt containing circular piers whose tremendous strength suggest that they must have upheld an enormous Romanesque church. The building was completed by 1123, but two hundred and forty years later the whole of St Mary's was rebuilt under the patronage of the Beauchamp Earls of Warwick. The family held the title from 1268 until 1445 – playing a great part in national affairs – and their effect upon Warwick is still to be seen, chiefly in the great strength of Warwick Castle and in the beauty

1

2

3

from head to foot.

The last and most magnificent phase of the medieval rebuilding was the erection of the chapel of Our Lady (6) – or the 'Beauchamp Chapel' as it later became known. Its founder was Richard Beauchamp, the fifth and most powerful Earl of that name, who completed the reconstruction project, begun by his father and grandfather, by the addition of this incomparable chapel to their great church. Richard's tomb (9) is at the very centre of the Perpendicular building he caused to be raised to receive it. He died in 1439 at Rouen, but had instructed, *I will*

4

5

of their church of St Mary.

It is not known why Thomas, the first Beauchamp Earl, pulled down the Norman building and started his own reconstruction on a larger and grander scale, but the Beauchamps' zestful pursuit of violence never checked their enthusiasm for ecclesiastical building. Thomas fought in all the French wars of King Edward III's reign, and commanded forces at the Battle of Crecy, at Poitiers and at the Siege of Calais – where he contracted the plague and died in 1369. From money received by the ransom of a French Archbishop he instigated the rebuilding programme at St Mary's, and his heir, another Thomas, continued his father's grand design. His brass (1) in the south transept is one of the finest examples of its kind, and shows the Earl encased in armour

that when it liketh God, that my Soule depart out of this World, my Body be interred within the Church Collegiate of our Lady of Warrwick, where I will, that in such place as I have devised (which is known well) that there be made a Chappell of Our Lady, well faire, and goodly

built, within the middle of which Chappell I will, that my Tomb be made'.

True to his behest the chapel was indeed *'well, faire and goodly built'* with only the finest of craftsmen contracted to build and embellish. The King's glazier, John Prudde, was charged to provide the windows and it was stipulated that he was only to use the best glass *'from beyond the seas'* – from Flanders. Sumptuous remains of the chapel glass (8) include the figures of Richard's favourite saints, St Thomas à Becket and the protomartyr St Alban, in which every known resource and

technique was utilised to achieve the most impressive effect. Coloured jewels were inserted into the borders of robes, and the feathered angels of the tracery hold real plainsong, which is still occasionally sung by mortals in the church. A carved reredos, oak clergy stalls, white walls, gilded mouldings and a beautiful vaulted ceiling (3), with bosses in colour and gold, complete the original scheme of opulence.

Richard Beauchamp, the Commander of Calais for King Henry V, was one of the hero-figures of the 15th century, but he reaches us today somewhat tainted

7

8   9

– as the man responsible for the imprisonment, interrogation, trial and execution of Joan of Arc. That pitiless act haunts the modern mind, but no such pangs of conscience afflicted his contemporaries, for any threat to the child-King Henry VI – whose protection was Richard's sacred trust – was, of necessity, ruthlessly suppressed. His tomb (2), constructed by John Borde in Purbeck marble, with an effigy (5) cast by William Austen of London, is one of the most beautifully sculpted in Europe – of such exquisite detail that even the veins of his temple are faithfully recorded. Its base is encircled by gilded statues, or 'weepers' (4), which occupy intricately carved niches. The monument is an excellent example of the strength and elegance of 15th century art in England – its controlled grandeur and authority is in dismissive contrast to the bombastic uncertainties of the Elizabethan tombs nearby.

ST PAULS/ST MARY-AT-HILL

Britain's only Classical Cathedral, St Paul's (1,3 and 4) in London, is also the only one conceived and completed by one man in the course of his own lifetime. Sir Christopher Wren's mission to rebuild St Paul's took thirty-six years, and its grandeur and sheer architectural brilliance are a towering monument to his genius.

The catastrophe of the Great Fire in 1666 put an end to one of the proudest medieval cathedrals of its age – whose nave and chancel were longer than any other in England, and whose spire (an almost unbelievable 489ft in height) was the tallest in Europe. The architectural scope for the rebuilding of St Paul's offered a unique opportunity to create an entirely new cathedral upon a virgin site – the first since Salisbury was founded four hundred and forty years beforehand. The classical idiom – the nearest that Protestant England ever came to the Baroque, with ornate gilded mosaics and saucer domes (4) –

used with such assured confidence suggests a break with the past, but St Paul's is, in fact, the traditional cathedral plan with twin-towered West Front and the central dominating feature over the crossing. Even though this latter feature is the magnificent imperial dome (and not a tower) the method used by the architect to poise the 68,000 ton downward thrust over the huge central space – eight enormous pillars (3) – was inspired by the Gothic precedent set by the octagon at Ely.

Within the burnt husk of the medieval ruin, Wren found a piece of shattered grave-slab upon which the solitary legend '*Resurgam*', '*I shall rise again*', was inscribed. In gratitude for the fulfilment of this prophecy, the finished building has a phoenix rising from the ashes of a funeral pyre carved above the entrance to the south transept.

■ Another Wren masterpiece, the church of **St Mary-at-Hill** (2), has a similar plan to that of his great cathedral – cruciform with a dome over the crossing. The plaster-work is in the Adam style, delicate and airy, which contrasts with the massive and splendid woodwork of the nave, pulpit and altar (2)– it being one of the loveliest and least spoilt interiors in the City.

SOMPTING/ST MARTHA-ON-THE-HILL

The Anglo-Saxons first came to Britain as pagan raiders about AD 400. Three centuries later they had peopled and tamed much of England. During this period the Saxons embraced Christianity, and although still divided into many kingdoms, they established a united Church. Their faith was to be the inspiration for their finest works of architecture. The tower of **Sompting Church** (4) in West Sussex has survived for a thousand years as evidence of their skill. The 100ft high tower is unique in England – being the only remaining example of the style known as the 'Rhenish Helm'. The

use of Roman bricks in the masonry at Sompting shows how Saxon England grew out of the ruins of Roman Britain.

■ Although a Norman church, **St Martha-on-the-Hill** (2) above the Pilgrim's Way in Surrey, is a Saxon foundation, raised upon the site of four 'Druid Circles' buried beneath the bracken on the south side of the hill. The church's dedication is a corruption of 'St Martyrs' – for upon this spot six hundred Christians were put to the sword in early Saxon times. In the centuries that followed the massacre prayers were raised for the souls of those slain, and in 1463 Bishop Waynflete of Winchester granted an indulgence of forty days to *'all those who came for devotion, prayers, pilgrimage or offering to the chapel; and should there recite the Paternoster, Angel's Salutation and Apostles' Creed'*. Still to be seen are the pilgrims' votive crosses incised into the stonework of the old nave doorway.

■ Similar medieval graffiti (although infinitely more extensive and interesting) exists at the magnificent 14th century church **St Mary's, Ashwell** (3 and 5) in Hertfordshire. On the north wall under the tower is a scratched Latin inscription (3) of great historical importance, *'M. CT. Expente miseranda ferox, violenta MCCLL'*. Translated into English, these tragic words mean *'1350 miserable, wild, distracted, the dregs of the people alone survive to witness...'* referring to the Black Death which swept through England killing one man in three. Another inscription alludes to the Magna Carta – *'Let the Church of England be free'*.

7

8

12

11

13

The richness of stained glass is an indication of the prosperity of a city or town in the Middle Ages. Florence, Chartres and York are typical of Italian, French and English cities that acquired their wealth of stained glass when their merchant classes were at their most affluent. The latter, a great wood centre, still has nineteen medieval parish churches, many rich in coloured glass – which is not surprisng since York was famous for its stained glass workshops. The most exciting windows (some eleven in all) are in **All Saints' Church, York** (6 -14). A particularly fine one, dating from

1410, depicts the 'Corporate Acts of Mercy'. Six of the compassionate deeds: giving drink to the thirsty (9), feeding the hungry, housing the stranger (10), clothing the naked (11), tending the sick (12) and visiting the imprisoned (13) still survive, but the seventh, burying the dead, is missing. Death dominates another of All Saints' famous windows. This is based upon a poem, *'The Prickle of Conscience'*, written in Northumbrian dialect by the mystic, Richard Rolle. The theme covers life, death, Purgatory, Doomsday, the pains of Hell and the bliss of Heaven. The window is

14

intended as a warning of what is to come and concentrates on the last fifteen days of the world. The macabre scenes are most vividly evoked, and include monsters emerging from the seas to overrun the land (7), the sea and trees on fire (8), the ground giving up the bones of the dead (6), men hiding in shelters to pray for help, death coming to claim all mortals, and finally, earthquakes and flames devouring everything on the last day.

■ 1: The north chancel of **Mottistone** church on the Isle of Wight.

DURHAM CATHEDRAL

Considered to be the world's supreme masterpiece of Romanesque architecture, the Anglo-Norman cathedral at **Durham** (1-12) could want for no finer setting. It dominates the lofty sandstone peninsula on which it rests (2), encircled by a great loop of the River Wear on all three sides, and guarded on its landward approach by a mighty Norman fortress. The strength of its position made Durham the '*Citadel of the Holy Church of the North*', shielding the sacred relics of St Cuthbert against the ravages of Scottish incursions and Viking raids. The saint's relics proved the inspiration for the founding of the cathedral

1540, but when the tomb was opened the Reformers found that his body – despite the passing of eight centuries – had remained in perfect condition, with no visible sign of decay. To the monks, however, it had been common knowledge that the saint's hair and nails continued to grow and, from time to time, it was necessary for the guardian of the shrine to open the tomb and trim the growth. At the discretion of the King's commissioners Durham's chief treasure was allowed to rest beneath the site of his once sumptuous shrine, under a slab of stone simply inscribed '*Cuthbertus*' (1,3 and 4).

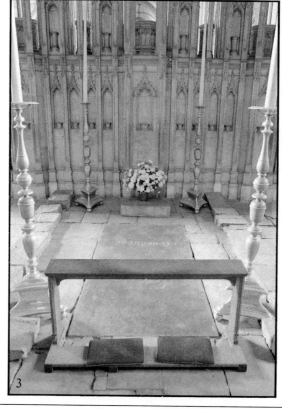

and his shrine became the 'brightest jewel of the north' – '*exalted with the most curious workmanship, of fine and costly green marble, all limned (painted) with gilt and gold; having four seats underneath the shrine for lame men to offer their devout and fervent prayer to God and Holy St Cuthbert, for his miraculous relief and succour which, being never wanting, made the shrine to be so richly invested with silver, gold, elephant tooth and suchlike things, that it was esteemed one of the most fabled monuments in all England*'. Of the many gifts that crowded the shrine, among the most unusual were part of Moses' rod, a fragment of Jesus' manger, a unicorn horn and the claw of a griffin with several of her eggs. Only men were admitted to the presence of the tomb as St Cuthbert appears to have developed an aversion to women which in medieval times resulted in the defining of a black marble boundary line in the nave, over which no female dared to tread. Cuthbert's shrine was despoiled in

DURHAM CATHEDRAL

The cathedral itself was raised during the period 1093 to 1133, and its abiding spirit is one of massive strength and overwhelming grandeur; yet despite its force, Durham is so well proportioned that nothing about it seems ponderous. The 201ft long nave (5) was considered the miracle of its day, and its lofty arcading is borne on alternating clustered piers (6 and 8) and massive circular columns – each boldly incised with swirling, almost barbaric, patterns of chevron (11), vertical flute and chequer pattern (9). Above the aisles, shadowed galleries (10) harbour England's

first flying buttresses. The cathedral is also the earliest building in Europe to have ribbed vaults throughout (7), and pioneered the use of the pointed arch to divide the nave into bays – a feature that was to be the secret of the world's greatest architecture – Durham is thus not merely the triumphant climax of Romanesque art, but also the first hint of the Gothic.

Few examples of Norman sculpture have survived which can compare with the savage splendour of Durham's bronze sanctuary knocker (12). The grotesque 'griffin head' mask (whose face once

6

7

8

9

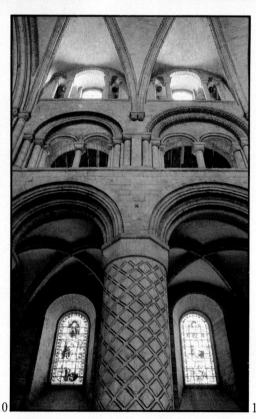

10

11

cathedral: he had to toll a special bell formally to signal his claim of sanctuary, confess his crime to a priest, surrender his arms and pay a nominal fee. Common law then allowed the fugitive the right to take an oath of 'abjuration of the realm', whereby (dressed in a long white robe and armed only with a crucifix) he had but nine days to quit the Kingdom.

■ The little Norman church near the abbey ruins at **Hailes** (15) in Gloucestershire is one of the most unspoilt in the country. Cement rendered on the outside, it perhaps does not look very interesting, but within everything is old. There is

Norman window. Beneath the foot of St Catherine lies the crowned head of the Emperor Maxentius whom she humiliated; and St Margaret is seen thrusting the shaft of a long-stemmed cross down the throat of Satan (in the guise of a dragon). Many of Hailes' tiles were brought to the church from the abandoned Cistercian abbey; and the oak canopied pulpit dates from the 17th century, as does much of the panelling and choir stalls. In the same county, St Mary's, **Upleadon** (13) is a 12th century church containing a fine Norman doorway which includes a sculptured tympanum. The superb

13

15

flashed with the fire of red enamel eyes) leers menacingly from the cathedral's great north door, yet would seem better suited to the prow of a Viking longship. Its frightening countenance was, however, a welcome sight to the eyes of debtors and fugitives

fleeing the terrifying excesses of medieval civil law. By clinging to the metal ring a criminal could claim the Right of Sanctuary (which dates back to the Old Testament). If he conformed to a strict code of conduct, the felon was permitted to shelter within the

medieval stained glass and a series of well preserved wall paintings of c1300 – including a representation of St Catherine of Alexandria and St Margaret of Antioch. The two saints often appear in each other's company and are painted together in the splays of a half-blocked

tower, with its pyramid cap, is of half-timbered construction and was raised in c1500.

■ The Perpendicular church of **Lustleigh** (14) has a granite tower contemporary to Upleadon and a lavishly carved mid-15th century screen.

LONG MELFORD/LAVENHAM

Two of the finest Perpendicular churches in the country, **Long Melford** (1) and **Lavenham** (4), owe their size and splendour to the prosperity of the 15th century, when Suffolk cloth was highly prized, and Suffolk wool was practically as valuable as gold (today the Lord Chancellor still sits on the Woolsack). Their well-proportioned towers emphasise the vertical lines of Perpendicular architecture and set the style for the rest of the church. Within, nave and chancel almost disappear in perspective, and an air of spaciousness pervades all. In characteristic fashion the walls are virtually 'sides of glass' and through their window tracery, and through that of the clerestory, light floods in, illuminating the church's many treasures – at Lavenham, the lovely Spring chantry chapel with its parclose screen around the tomb of its founder – a wealthy clothier who paid for the steeple – and at Long Melford the brasses of the Clopton family and, directly behind the high altar, the vestry

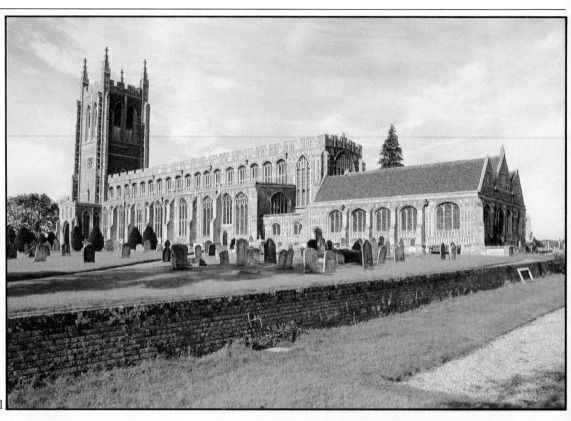

and marvellous Lady chapel, surrounded by an ambulatory.

■ The church of **St Clement Danes** (2 and 3) has stood on its site in the Strand since the 9th century; and it is said that when King Alfred expelled the Danes from London those who had English wives were permitted to remain in the area – hence St Clement (of the) Danes. The original church was rebuilt in Norman times, and again in the Middle Ages. It escaped the flames of the Great Fire, but became unsafe in 1680 and was demolished and rebuilt again by

Sir Christopher Wren. He recased the medieval tower with new stone and surmounted it with obelisks. The spire – which houses the famous peal of eleven bells that ring out the well known tune '*oranges and lemons*' – was added in the 18th century by Gibbs. The interior (2) is striking – black oak predominates up to the height of the gallery, whilst above, all is brightness and light, in white, grey and gold. The panelled ceiling is supported by elegant columns which lead the eye down the body of the church to the richly gilded focal point of the high altar (3).

STOKE D'ABERNON

The church of St Mary at **Stoke D'Abernon** (1,2,3,4 and 5) is one of the oldest in the Kingdom. It was built in the latter part of the 7th century and belongs, with a scattered group of other south-eastern churches, to the period immediately following St Augustine's mission to Kent in AD 597. Substantial portions of the original fabric survive on the south side; and Stoke D'Abernon is the earliest English example of a church which had a thegn's gallery, or Lord's seat – the doorway to which is positioned 12 ft above ground level, and was once reached by a wooden stairway. The portal is

now bricked-in, but its megalithic structure can still be clearly seen in the south wall of the nave.

After five hundred years without alteration the Normans added the north aisle c1190. The chancel, with its exceptionally fine quadripartite vault – which has a carved and gilded rose (the emblem of the Virgin, to whom the church is dedicated) at its centre – was raised in the 13th century. Within the chancel is the magnificent brass of Sir John D'Abernon, dated 1277 and acknowledged to be the oldest brass now remaining in England. Other treasured possessions include an imposing late-Elizabethan walnut pulpit of Mannerist design, and a 12th century chest which was probably one of those ordered to be made and placed in all churches in 1199 to collect alms for the Crusade. There is also a handsome and unusual Jacobean oak lectern in the form of a gilded eagle (2), and much notable stained glass – especially of pieces concerned with

BRAUNTON

the Blessed Virgin Mary. In the north transept is an English panel of c1520, but with Flemish influence, depicting the 'Burial of the Virgin' (1) – a rare subject in Art – matched with a French panel of 1540 representing 'The Angel appearing to the Shepherds' (4). These treasures that the church shelters are augmented by the beauty of its exterior – of its ancient walls of large field-flints embowered in ivy and shady trees (3), positioned by the banks of the lovely and deep-flowing River Mole (5).

■ The church of **Braunton** (6,7,8 and 9) was founded at an even earlier date than that of the Surrey church of Stoke D'Abernon. Its first timbers were raised at least thirty years before Pope Gregory

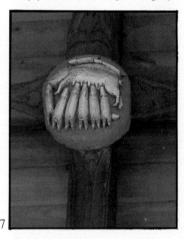

despatched St Augustine to convert England to the Faith, by St Brannock, the son of a king of Calabria, who evangelised South Wales and spent many years engaged in missionary work for the Celtic church in North Devon. Here, at Braunton, he was instructed in a vision to build his minster at the site where he would find a white sow and her farrow: the legend is commemorated by one of the bosses of the medieval roof (7). He died in Wales in the year AD 570, and his remains were brought back to the church of his foundation and are almost certainly buried beneath the high altar.

The present church dates mostly from the 13th century, with a massive Norman tower, topped by a lead-shingled broach spire. The remarkably wide nave (6) is spanned by a fine wagon-roof, and there is a splendid collection of carved, 16th century bench-ends – one of which possesses a sculpture of the church's patron, St Brannock (8), and another displays the 'Instruments of the Passion' (9).

The parish church of **St Mary Redcliffe** in Bristol (1,2,3,4 and 6) is accredited universally as one of the finest examples of Gothic architecture in Europe. The opinion most commonly quoted is that of Queen Elizabeth I who, on her visit to the church in 1574, described it as '*the fairest, goodliest and most famous parish church in England*'. It is distinguished first and foremost by its size and plan, which are almost those of an abbey. St Mary's contains distinguished work from the early-13th to 15th century, the best being that of the late-14th century.

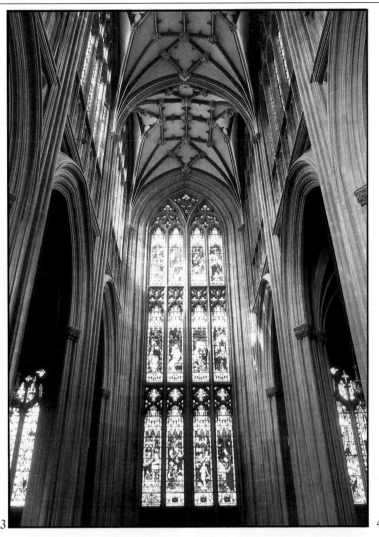

The munificence of local merchants whose fortunes were amassed by trading fleets based at the nearby harbour (John and Sebastian Cabot, the discoverers of Newfoundland, being notable patrons) contributed to the architectural embellishment of the medieval church. It was during this period that St Mary's achieved its greatest glory, and it is hard to conceive of anything more gracious than the piers of the nave (1) and clerestory – where the absence of capitals gives added delicacy to the pillars by allowing the line from the floor to vault to remain unbroken –

or anything more beautiful than the roof, with its lierne vaulting of tufa rubble (2), with which almost the entire church is covered. The bosses of the vault are especially fine – there are more than one thousand two hundred of them, all different, and each one covered in pure gold. In the south transept (3) – which is architecturally interesting for the rare distinction of possessing double aisles – are some of the loveliest roof bosses, whose gilding was added in 1740 when the women of the city donated their gold jewellery to be melted down.

In marked contrast to the tower of St Mary Redcliffe (6) – richly decorated and soaring for 285ft - is the three-storey, pagoda-type tower of the Priory Church of St Laurence, **Blackmore** (5) built of local oak in the 15th century. Only by careful study of these timbers can one fully appreciate the strength and beauty of the tower's construction, and the skill with which medieval craftsmen selected and handled their materials.

5

6

BRIXWORTH

All Saints' Church, **Brixworth** (1,3,6 and 7), built some two or three hundred years after the Romans left Britain, is without question the most impressive and outstanding early-Saxon building in the country. Not only is it one of the few constructions to have survived from the 7th century almost complete (6); but it has been in continuous use as a centre of Christian worship from its inception to the present day – a

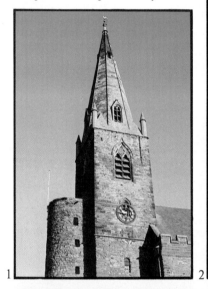

span of thirteen hundred years. Indeed, its present impressive size is now actually smaller than when the original minster was constructed.

Brixworth is built of stone rubble with a substantial amount of Roman tiles utilised in the abaci, the arches (7) and in portions of the tower. When the minster church was founded it must have proved a suitable centre from which to spread the Gospel to the

heathen tribes of Mercia; and the narthex at the west end (part of which survives in the tower) was used for the instruction of *catechumens* – converts under instruction in the Faith.

The reddened stones at the west end of the church are an indication of severe heat, and such burning would agree with the theory that Brixworth was sacked by Danes in the early years of its history. During subsequent rebuilding work in the

late-9th and early-10th centuries, part of the existing sanctuary and the vaulted stair turret were built against the tower (1). The latter houses a good example of a helical staircase centered on a newel post, which permits access to the tower's upper chamber. This room has a window looking into the nave and was used – as at its fellow Northamptonshire church, Earls Barton – by persons of distinction. From this window, with its lovely baluster shafts, one can inspect the intricacies of the nave's roof construction (3) and the interplay of king-posts and tie-beams.

Various alterations were made in the Middle Ages: the Lady chapel was built in the 13th century, and the belfry and spire raised in 1350. There is also an ancient, sunken ring-crypt beneath the apse, where stood the sacred relic of the throat bone of the great preacher St Boniface. To prevent it being

6

7

8

desecrated during the Reformation the last chantry priest of Brixworth, Thomas Bassenden, bricked up the treasure in the Lady chapel wall where it was uncovered three hundred years later. This priceless relic is now displayed within a heavy iron cage in the reliquary.

■ The Doomsday Book church of St Peter and St Paul **Albury** (2,4,5 and 8) in Surrey, is beautifully situated in a well timbered park, but has been disused since 1842. It has traces of Saxon stone-work, and the tower – whose interior (8) is lit by pre-Conquest windows – is part Saxon, part Norman, and is surmounted by a 17th century cupola (2). The chancel is a ruin, but the south transept was lavishly remodelled by Augustus Pugin in the early 1840s as a mortality chapel of the Drummond Family. The feel of this chapel is vividly Victorian, with stained glass by William Wailes (5) and walls and ceiling elaborately decorated in heraldry (4), coloured and gilded by Thomas Earle.

BARTON-UPON-HUMBER/RAUNDS

St Peter's at **Barton-upon-Humber** (4) in Lincolnshire, is an example of the curious Saxon plan in which the tower forms the body of the church, with a tiny chapel projecting towards the east. The noble pre-Conquest tower (4) dates from the 10th century, with earlier foundations which may go back to the original missionary church of St Chad, built in the 8th century. The general impression made by the tall, square, unbuttressed structure, so delicately patterned by its rows of arcading – the lower round-arched, the upper triangular-headed – is emphatically linear. The windows are small and occur in pairs, both lights being divided

sacred monogram I.H.S. – *'Iesus Hominum Salvator'* (Jesus the Saviour of Mankind) – to indicate the mural's former glory.

■ The City of London's church of **St Mary Aldermary** (2) was first mentioned in the 11th century, and was rebuilt after the Great Fire by Wren – the money being donated on condition that the new building echoed the architectural principles of the old, medieval church. Thus, the aisles and nave are charmingly roofed in Wren's own version of late-Perpendicular fan vaulting (2), consisting of circular saucer domes and semicircles with the spaces in between filled with quatrefoil panelling.

by a heavy, central shaft.

■ Noted for its ornate, 133ft high tower and Northamptonshire broach spire, the Early English church of St Peter at **Raunds** (1,3 and 5) possesses an elegant and well-proportioned nave (3) famous for its vigorous 15th century wall-paintings that adorn the northern arcade below the clerestory. The murals depict the 'Three Living and the Three Dead', a mortality picture on the vanity of life – three kings in rich robes encounter skeleton kings who mock earthly 'treasures'. There is also a fascinating study of a saint harried by demons (1), and an excellent example of the theme of the 'Seven Deadly Sins'. Above the chancel arch (5) a painting of Calvary prepared medieval worshippers for the sanctity of the Mass. Sadly the crucified figure of Christ and the supporting witnesses to His suffering, the Virgin Mary and St John the Baptist, are defaced, but enough remains in the representation of the Evangelists and the repeated

Near the site of the parish church of St Mary at **North Elmham** (1,3,4 and 5) stand the ruins of a Saxon cathedral founded in the 7th century. The diocese covered the whole of East Anglia, but the bishopric was removed to Thetford in 1071, and from there transferred to Norwich in 1095. The bishops continued to cherish their link with North Elmham and such was their love for the little village, which had once been the centre of their See, that they endowed it with a magnificent medieval church.

St Mary's was raised by the first Norman Bishop of Norwich,

on her head, and carries a garland of flowers in her hand.

■ **Blisland Church** (2) in Cornwall – dedicated to St Portus and St Hyacinth – is celebrated for its coloured and intricately carved rood-screen, the work of F.C. Eden in 1894. As a restoration (even improvement) of a medieval church this can hardly be bettered. The screen, with its 10ft high Calvary carved in Oberammergau, Bavaria, is how most of the West Country and East Anglian medieval rood-screens would have looked in their youth.

■ **Kilpeck** (6 and 7) in Herefordshire, owes its universal

1

Bishop de Losinga, at the beginning of the 12th century, and substantially remodelled one hundred years later when the Romanesque arcade was replaced by the present alternating round and octagonal piers and capitals of the early-Gothic style. The chancel (5) dates from the late-13th century and the impressive square tower from c1400. The tower walls differ from the rest of the church (1) in that they are faced with rough flintwork, in contrast to the knapped flints used elsewhere.

Within the church, North Elmham's chief features are its bench-ends with poppyhead carving, and the surviving lower part of its early-14th century rood-screen, containing some of the best and earliest screen painting in the country. The faces of the sixteen panels have been scratched, but the saints can be identified from the symbols they bear: St Thomas (3) holds a spear – the instrument of his martyrdom – and St Cecilia (4), the patron saint of music, wears a wreath of roses and lilies

3

4

In the tympanum is a formalised Tree of Life bearing thick grapes. The outer arch of the portal has linked medallions of mythical monsters, fish, birds, a lion with a man's face, a phoenix in flames, and dragons swallowing each other with such abandon that the final dragon is swallowing itself. Two Welsh warriors – wearing mail jerkins and Phrygian caps – on the left-hand column, are said to represent both Church and State.

A corbel table embraces the whole building with a wealth of carvings, and over the portal is depicted the 'Holy Lamb of God', the only religious sculpture, for the rest of the eighty figures are symbols of the chase – falcons, harts and wild boar heads. Other motifs include a dog and rabbit, wrestlers, a sheila-na-gig, a muzzled bear and a ram's head: evidently some of these figures were considered too erotic in detail and were removed during Victorian restoration work.

Many widely differing influences have come together at

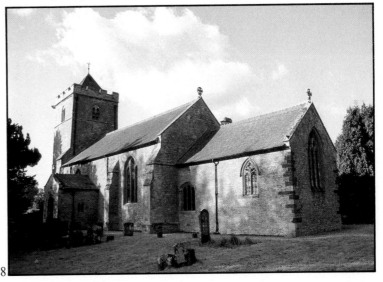

acclaim to its small Norman church – the most perfectly preserved and, architecturally, the richest example of its kind in England. Apart from a corner of the nave, which is Saxon, and some late-medieval windows, everything in the church dates from the third quarter of the 12th century. The whole exterior is rich in Romanesque decoration, yet the gem is without doubt the sumptuously carved southern doorway (7). Here is depicted 'Eden', the Temptation and the Fall of Man who, on the right-hand jamb, is represented as being tempted to eat the forbidden fruit of the knowledge of good and evil.

Kilpeck. The arches of the portal and the beakheads of the corbel table are said to have drawn their inspiration from manuscripts kept in the great Benedictine Abbey at Reading: the figures of warriors are clearly Celtic (Kilpeck was very much in Wales during the 12th century) and the long, twisting *gragons*, or serpents, are purely Viking – like nothing so much as figureheads of wooden ships, they could have been lifted straight from the prow of a Viking longship.

■ 8: The remote country church at **Leckhampstead** in Buckinghamshire, dedicated to the Assumption of the Blessed Virgin.

ST PETER, MANCROFT

Norwich is reputed to have more medieval churches – thirty-two in all – than any other city north of the Alps. Of these **St Peter Mancroft** (1,2,3,4,5,6,8,9 and 11) is incomparably the finest. Indeed, it has few rivals among the parish churches of England for its unity and beauty. Even John Wesley – with his preference for an open-air altar – wrote of St Peter's in his diary, '*I scarcely remember ever to have seen a more beautiful parish church; the more so because its beauty results not from foreign ornaments, but from the very fine form and structure of it. It is very large, and of uncommon height, and venerable look, and at the same time surprisingly cheerful*'.

Upon entering the splendid Perpendicular church one is immediately aware of the nobility of its proportions and the unity of its design; a legacy of its completion within a single period, 1430-55. The whole 180ft length of its interior (1) is quite staggering in size, but all can be taken in at one glance; there is no chancel arch to

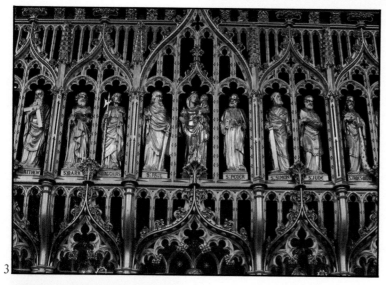

break the vista eastwards (6) and the eight bays of the aisle arcade march from end to end. Looking at this elegant arcade one wonders that such piers, so tall and widely spaced, can support the great arches, with their walls above – pierced by continuous rows of clerestory windows (2) – and crowning all, the heavy vault of chancel and nave which one knows to be topped with lead. It is a hammer-beam and arch-braced roof (8) – one of St Peter's greatest glories – but the hammer-beams are concealed under the beautiful fan-like groining (9); this in turn rests on long wall posts supported

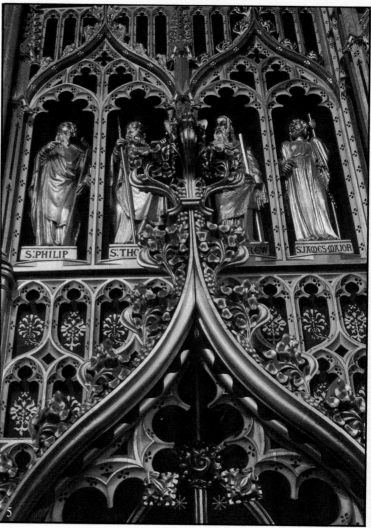